Reflections from a Moving Stream

A Collection of Poems

Pratap Jayavanth

notionpress.com

INDIA · SINGAPORE · MALAYSIA

ISBN
Hardcase 979-8-89632-409-6
Paperback 979-8-89610-291-5

This collection of poems is affectionately dedicated to my mother, Amritha Ranjini Raju who lives in New Zealand. A multi-talented person, she continues to be a source of inspiration to all her family members including her children, grandchildren, great grandchildren and numerous friends. A devoted home-maker, an intrepid globe-trotter, an excellent cook, a multi-skilled artist, and in-house champion in carroms, scrabble, crosswords and Sudoku; she is truly amazing!

At one time, Ranjini was one of the oldest persons in Auckland to practice Tai Chi. She was brought up in the Christian tradition; her father, Rev. Gopalaswamy was a missionary and her mother, Smt. Rajamma, was a deeply religious lady. Ranjini's strong positive attitude in life is clearly reflected in the family motto she promotes, "I am getting better day by day in every way"!

National Bird of India

(Source: Pixabay)

CONTENTS

WHAT'S IN A TITLE

"Reflections from a Moving Stream" has a deeper meaning, that nothing is permanent or static. There is an emphasis on transition either through time, travel or thoughts. These delicate threads are poetically woven into the sensitive fabric of the compositions in this book.

Conceptualized and documented over several decades, this collection represents poetically proactive and philosophically provocative "pearls of wisdom"! All are influenced by contextual anecdotes, personal interactions, global events, and divine experiences!

The title for this book touches on individual perceptions; what one person sees in a moving stream depends on where one is standing and what one is looking at. One day, it could be a transparent blue sky above with clouds floating by; on another day, a slow procession of ducks and the ripples on the water!

On this side of the bank, it could be the tall, sturdy trees gently dancing in the wind. Or on the other side, elderly people taking an early morning stroll, immersed in their own philosophical rationalization of events!

ACKNOWLEDGEMENTS

I wish to acknowledge with a deep sense of gratitude, the encouragement from family and friends who literally pushed me to publish my collection of poems. 'Reflections from a Moving Stream' was first published in 2021 and presented to my mother on her ninety-fifth birthday. Copies were gifted to family and close friends for their reading pleasure.

My sincere thanks to Sukheshini Grandhi for the cover photo. Credits for other contributions (in alphabetical order) go to- Abhitha Naidu, Arun Chinnikrishna, Deepak Jayavant, Kala Jayavant, Kiran Jayavanth, Ramisetty Venkata Rama and Suravinda Chennam. Most of the images are from Pixabay and a few photos were taken by me.

The current edition with additional poems is published under an agreement with Notion Press Media Private Limited. I am indeed grateful to the literary team of Notion Press for their excellent technical assistance.

Section-A: Spiritually Scripted

- My Mother
- Why God Came Down
- Science Vs Spirituality
- Live Well, Live Longer
- Strangers can also be Friends
- Survival Kit

MY MOTHER

As a baby, I cannot just remember,
The number of times, my Mother,
Thoughtfully trimmed my tiny nails,
So I don't scratch my newborn face!

Nor can I recollect the many times,
I must have cried, and cried aloud,
But her sweet ever-loving patience,
Mystically quelled the night storm!

But this, I certainly can never forget,
The time I had the itchy chicken pox,
Her soothing wave with *neem* leaves,
Day and night, was a heavenly balm!

Now I know, even a thousand angels,
Cannot ever replace a mother's love,
God, with infinite wisdom, and grace,
Has blessed everyone, with a Mother!

WHY GOD CAME DOWN

In His plan on earth, God designed,
And created in His image, mankind,
That they remain above all creations,
And live in peace with other nations!

Harsh footpaths over hills on our way,
Some across plains, lest we go astray,
Few face wild beasts in a dense jungle,
God tests our faith to see if we bungle!

Once silent streams join one another,
They turn into a mighty river altogether,
Then flow majestically towards the sea,
Shaped by the Lord to merge, ego-free!

Though, many defied and paid the price,
God sent His Saints to save us from vice,
Finally, He Himself, descended on earth,
To adoringly forgive us for all our worth!

SCIENCE *VERSUS* SPIRITUALITY

Scientific principles verified and tested,
But spiritual teachings always disputed,
Former uses the mind; latter, the heart,
Are Science and Spirituality, truly apart?

Ignorance is bliss, for frogs in the well,
Not for thinkers, wherever they dwell,
Knowledge-seekers will find the truth,
And unravel a mystery like any sleuth!

Blessed are those on a heavenly flight,
Over spiritual darkness, they saw light,
Yet, a doubting Thomas, here or there,
Remains unconvinced, ready to swear!

Divine manifestations aligned to belief,
Are God's promise to give humans relief,
Mystified scientists offer no explanation,
As miracles are beyond comprehension!

LIVE WELL, LIVE LONGER!

Often people pray for happiness and wealth,
Do we pause to look at our body and health?
Even for better career and position to boast,
Ever think of God's gift of life at every toast?

Festivals in many nations offer a lavish feast,
Yielding shyly to temptations to say the least,
Mouth-watering delicacies laid on your plate,
And you lose the battle to watch your weight!

Gastronomically prone are wary of junk food,
And chose what's healthy to elevate the mood,
Exercise restraint as they read the menu card,
And within the limits, stay fit like any die hard!

The secret for longer life is so simple to follow,
"Eat half, walk double, laugh triple" isn't hollow,
Also don't forget to add 'love without measure',
It's an old Tibetan proverb that I wish to share!

STRANGERS CAN ALSO BE FRIENDS!

The journey of life is stranger than fiction,
Meeting new folks without any prediction,
Absolute strangers become friends forever,
Close friends leave for motives whatsoever.

Blood relatives take their battles to court,
Use lawyers to claw at each other's throat,
Kith & kin lose the chance to live in peace,
But, peace will come when life does cease.

Often, when we travel in a bus, or a train,
Or seated next to a stranger on the plane,
A smiling 'Hi' may elicit a friendly reaction,
Or end briefly, with no further attraction!

Imagine an episode predestined to ensue,
Bonding a relationship without much ado,
With a stranger who becomes a soul-mate,
Surely it's a God-incidence, not simply fate!

SURVIVAL KIT

Survival is a challenge for one and all,
Faith is needed when against the wall,
God alone knows what's best for you,
Every believer will verify that it's true!

He has blessed us with unique DIY kit,
Divinely crafted for your individual fit,
Assemble with prayer and meditation,
Connect direct to Him in any situation!

The heavenly bank maintains account,
Selfless deeds enhance divine amount,
Invest in love bonds for lasting benefit,
Win God's grace, more than a megabit!

Always boost your Wi-Fi that's inbuilt,
Prevent earthly virus and shun conflict,
Receive His updates & avoid shutdown,
One day, you'll be a gem in His Crown!

Section-B: Nostalgically Noticeable

- Long, Long Ago
- Goodbye Dear Postman
- A Slice of Nostalgia
- Will Good Old Days Return?

LONG, LONG AGO…

Long, long ago…
No smoke from factories, no motor cars either,
Only cattle power to take us hither and thither,
A breath of fresh air had oxygen that was pure,
Now, with air pollution, not anymore for sure.

Long, long ago…
Fruits & vegetables were fresh from the farm,
Now preserved with chemicals, do more harm,
Same is the story with rice, lentils, and wheat,
Producers in the food chain prepared to cheat.

Long, long ago…
Water for drinking was straight from the well,
Now through reverse osmosis, well set to sell,
Ground water, for all the living, is best source,
But, industrial waste has changed that course.

Long, long ago…
Folks never heard of hazards from radiation,
No laptop, mobile, microwave, or television,
Our environment altered by every discovery,
Does God have a celestial plan for recovery?

GOODBYE DEAR POSTMAN

When was the last time…?
You saw a Postman cycling down your street,
Even on rainy days, never one to miss his beat,
The familiar cycle bell will ring near your gate,
Hurry, collect your mail, don't make him wait!

When was the last time…?
You wrote with your own fountain pen, a letter,
To a loved one, or an ailing friend to get better,
Or an aerogram to a dear pen friend overseas,
And walked to a Mailbox to keep mind at ease!

When was the last time…?
You skillfully removed the lovely foreign stamp,
After it's moistened; then eliminated the damp,
To stick another to your album, and felt proud,
Showing off to classmates & rest of the crowd!

When was the last time…?
You received from a Postman, a Money Order,
Was it from home to pay the fees as a boarder?
For money transfer, it was safe, and also swift,
Likewise, the only way to send a monetary gift!

When was the last time…?
You mailed a letter to a dear one at the border,
Just a name and code, rest was left to the sorter,
Heart-breaking moments & the agonizing wait,
Vanished when you saw a postman at the gate!

When was the last time…?
You went to a Post Office to send a telegram,
The Morse code, even faster than aerogram,
Good or bad, news quickly sent to any town,
The obliging Post Master won't let you down!

When was the last time…?
You heard a Postman ring the bell at midnight,
And loudly bellow, "Telegram", creating fright,
Amidst fears & prayers bonding the household,
The message was read by one who was bold!

Background: The poet recalls his childhood days spent at his grandparents' ancestral estate in Madras, South India.

A SLICE OF NOSTALGIA

Let me walk you down Gopal Street,
To a sylvan plantation that was neat,
Where stood a God-blessed cottage,
My grandpa called it the Hermitage!

A king-size fig tree secured the gate,
For birds, its fruits were yummy bait,
Swaying stately were coconut trees,
Like giant fans bringing cool breeze!

Summertime, we came for a reason,
That's the time of the mango season,
Granny put them to ripen on the hay,
And gave us luscious ones each day!

When the great circus came to town,
Most amusing of all was a tiny clown,
What animals did too, were amazing,
But trapeze acts, utterly hair-raising!

Evenings at the famous Marina Beach,
Stomping into the waves within reach,
Making sandcastles, picking sea shells,
Licking stick ice-cream had no parallels!

WILL GOOD OLD DAYS RETURN?

Once upon a time...
Welcome or send off attracted family and friends like flocks,
Today, terse messages with emoticons crowd your mailbox!
Once upon a time...
Birthdays were much awaited occasions for family & friends,
Today, it's greetings, cakes & floras online to make amends!

Once upon a time...
Invitations for weddings went to almost everyone connected,
Today, destination weddings invite those discretely selected!
Once upon a time...
Summer holidays at grandparents' home were truly exciting,
Today, video call from family in a far-off country is the thing!

Once upon a time...
I liked flying big kites, letting it go higher into the blue skies,
Today, my grandson operates a drone to do stunts as it flies!
Once upon a time...
My friends and I enjoyed playing with marbles after school,
Today, kids use iPad to play similar games, as per the rule!

Once upon a time...
We liked climbing trees, swaying like Tarzan & feeling tall,
Today, there's state-of-the-art wall-climbing in every Mall!
Once upon a time...
When it rained, it was either Snakes and Ladder, or Ludo,
Today, children can play outdoor sports on TV with gusto!

Once upon a time...
The warm feeling of sharing meals as a family was the norm,
Today, the microwave ensures at least the food stays warm!
Once upon a time...
Relationships were ardently shielded and remained forever,
Today, unpredictable, rapidly break for reasons whatsoever!

Once upon a time...
There was plenty of faith in God and plenty of time for prayer,
Today, time for everything except God, thus ending in despair!

National Heritage Animal of India

(Source: Pixabay)

Section-C: Puzzling Pandemic

- Battle-Scarred Veteran's Missing Medal
- Long Live, Frontline Warriors
- Confusion Worse Confounded
- My Sixth Sense
- Return of the Migrants
- Coping with Difficult Times
- If Colors Could Speak

Background: The poet was diagnosed with COVID pneumonia in May 2021. This poem expresses a COVID survivor's gratitude to God for being there in the hospital all the time and for orchestrating his miraculous and rapid recovery.

BATTLE-SCARRED VETERAN'S MISSING MEDAL

The antiquated radar picked up feeble signals,
the decoder failed to estimate the danger levels.
Waves of alien viral mutants from all directions,
skyjack airborne routes to nosedive on targets.
Surreptitiously invade moist alleys and airways,
breaking into alveoli to trigger immune responses,
destroying vital supply lines and oxygen reserves.
A battle-scarred veteran calls for reinforcement,
an urgent SOS first to the Supreme Commander.
All the generals on the ground immediately respond,
aerial units swiftly restore oxygen supply to normal,
subterranean channels ship life-saving medications,
soldiers in PPE check vital signs, deliver vitamins.
A fortnight later, the veteran hears the bugle at dawn,
war is over, victory declared; he is ready to join duty.
Battle-scarred survivor proudly eyes his war medals,
one that's missing is with His Supreme Commander!

Background: During the peak of the pandemic many front-line health workers lost their lives taking care of COVID-19 patients.

LONG LIVE, FRONTLINE WARRIORS!

They cared for them day and night,
Whispering softly to ease their pain,
Not anxious about their own plight,
Rather kept others alert and sane.

Attacking a foe hitherto unknown,
With an arsenal imperfect and old,
That seized all aged and full blown,
Even with remedies new and bold.

From north to south, east to west,
Scientists looked for ultimate cure,
Tried and tested, all that was best,
Some had success, others not sure.

Race for vaccines fast and furious,
Triggered off a geo-political sprint,
Left die-hards baffled and curious,
Globally laboratories faced a stint!

Most frontline warriors remained firm,
Only God saw their tireless obligation,
And summoned them before their term,
Was it a reward for selfless dedication?

Background: This poem captures the chaos and the confusion that partially surrounds the production, distribution and the utilization of the vaccines against the COVID-19 pandemic.

CONFUSION WORSE CONFOUNDED

Scientists, looked upon as superhuman,
Likely to offer solution for any situation,
Usually praised for their unique acumen,
Sometimes, get caught in a confusion.

Countries at the mercy of the COVID-19,
Fraught with cases and fragile economy,
Forced to increase production of vaccine,
Matching political pressure and autonomy.

When vaccines develop at amazing speed,
On technologies not used in humans before,
Entail extra-caution to safely meet the need,
Instead, set off confusion on what to explore.

Never before have scientists been so divided,
On how to control alarming surge in numbers,
Not only C-19 positives, but also, those dead,
Misinformation must stop to prevent blunders!

Background: Pets are not only adorable and loyal to man but also exhibit feelings in their own peculiar way. Dog lovers know!

MY SIXTH SENSE

My ears twitched and nostrils flared,
I knew for sure something is wrong,
My master appeared sick and scared,
Always saw him healthy and strong.

At once I barked and all were awake,
I saw an ambulance outside our gate,
Difficult for all to bear the heartache,
They took him away as if already late.

Strange to see everyone with a mask,
Washing their hands again and again,
Sat in a corner as I was given no task,
Missed my master and felt the pain.

One fine day, heard the horn of our car,
Knew for sure it was him coming home,
Wagging with joy leapt on him from far,
Happy that now we can go out to roam!

Background: Cross-border labor migration between India and Nepal is a regular phenomenon. During the lock down, thousands of labor migrants became suddenly jobless. They faced unimaginable suffering and hardship on their long return journey living under the open sky, without access to health care.

RETURN OF THE MIGRANTS

With sore feet and cracked heels,
Aching shoulder and empty belly,
Thousands march without wheels,
Few wept when they saw on telly.

Poor workers see no access to aid,
As the government shuts one eye,
Help is needed before hopes fade,
Only the kindhearted hear the cry.

The poor have struggled from birth,
Will the rich have a heart to share?
Will God's kingdom come on earth?
To ensure neighborly love and care?

COPING WITH DIFFICULT TIMES

Epidemiologists shake their heads in disbelief,
Viruses are defiant, mutants gain upper hand,
While those affected want a miraculous relief,
A pitiless pandemic turns a killer in every land.

The best scientists fail to counter the onslaught,
But two-faced leaders achieve political mileage,
Leaving their followers helpless and distraught,
While GPs struggle to update their knowledge.

It's Greek and Latin to patients utterly confused,
But kith and kin cautiously google for a solution,
Even as many families are bereaved and bruised,
The intrusive media always adds its contribution.

The R&D industries compete for the ultimate shot,
However, *"precautions better than cure"* is still effective,
Nevertheless, the *"variants of concern"* must be fought,
Divine mediation may ensure efforts are collective!

IF COLORS COULD SPEAK

Hi Doc, I will bet many don't know,
Colors can't speak but usually glow,
While Covid was simply another flu,
PPE became yellow, white and blue!

Many an accident, traffic lights avert,
Similar colors in each and every alert,
Like cars screech to halt when it's red!
Covid patients confined to stay in bed!

Isolated ones in orange were negative,
Hoping that RAT won't become positive,
Those in purple were happy with a friend,
A colorful period, but when will it end?

Public Health, urgently in the limelight,
As GPs and nurses toiled past midnight,
Contact tracing became order of the day,
As online business became a child's play!

In white masks, like aliens from the moon,
Folks waited fearfully for the news at noon,
Even with the tight security at every port,
Covid just breezed in without a passport!

Section-D: Medically Motivated

- Genesis
- The Oath
- An Enigma
- Time to Retire
- Happy Birthday
- DOSE for Happiness
- Friendly Fire
- The Tree of Life
- A Silent Truce

Background: Tremendous advances in technology have given us amazing information about the stages of development from the one-celled zygote to a multi-million-celled infant at the time of delivery. Previous generations did not have these facilities to know about life before birth. Human embryologists have stated that "the embryo is a human being from the time of fertilization because of its human chromosomal constitution and the zygote is the beginning of a developing human". Every human being however, is a distinct individual.

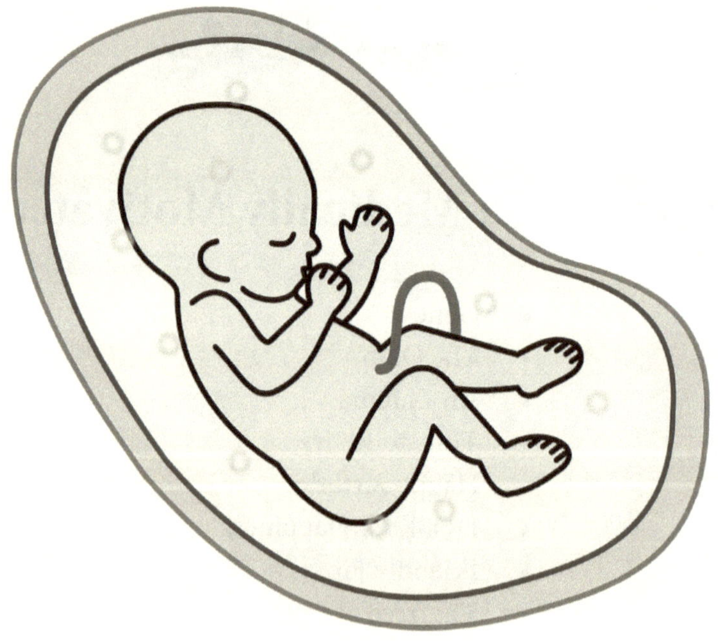

(Source: Pixabay)

GENESIS

Floating blissfully in a time capsule,
Comfortable in warm togetherness,
Surrounded by rich pulsating music,
From microscopic genesis to maturity.

The river of life ensures sustenance,
Indeed, an intricate mathematical wonder,
Involves not only addition but also division,
And multiplication to achieve replication.

And subtraction along with degeneration,
Simply to produce a chip of the old block,
History and geography mixed together,
Brought closer by an element of chance.

From different generations lost in the past,
When genetic components join each other,
Or worse, by some Mendelian inheritance,
Play a significant role in the final analogy.

Does zodiac science govern the deliveries?
When either by vertex, breech or caesarian,
Singletons, twins, triplets, maybe octuplets,
Arrive spontaneously or as an emergency!

Background: Hippocrates (c. 460–377 BC), Greek physician, is regarded as the Father of Medicine. For centuries, the medical profession has taken the Hippocrates' Oath and continues to do so. A doctor's duty is to save the life of a patient, even if it is the life of a convict waiting to be executed shortly. As a young doctor, the poet, had to treat a serial killer who was later sentenced to death.

(Source: Pixabay, image by Gordon Johnson)

THE OATH

The never-ending queue stretched my patience,
The packed noisy OPD, just like any other day,
Malingerers, hypochondriacs, also real patients,
Many get medicines, others tactfully sent away.

No sooner the last patient picked his prescription,
I had a weird feeling that the day is not yet over,
Alerted by the voices outside and the commotion,
I stifle a yawn, stretch my legs, as it draws closer.

On a stretcher encircled by cops is a wounded guy,
But needs no introduction, thanks to the television,
Helpless and lost, yet scornfully looked into my eye,
Bound to the Oath, I treated him with compassion.

Today, doctors will save him with the best treatment,
Unbiased though he killed two doctors in their prime,
The court duly awarded him the capital punishment,
Shortly, he would be hanged for that dreadful crime.

Background: This poem relates to a condition called, 'Facial Palsy' also known as Bell's Palsy, which is characterized by weakness of the muscles on one side of the face. It sums up the fact that for any medical condition, there could be a number of alternate explanations, and even the treatment needs to be tailored accordingly, in contrast to text book recommendations.

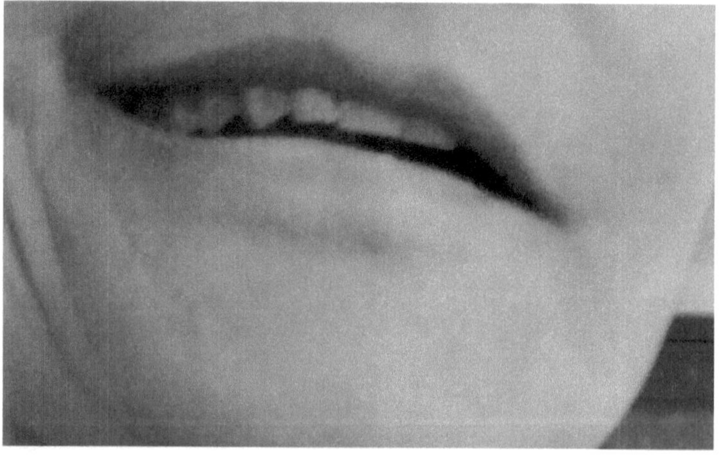

Source: RVR

AN ENIGMA

Medical students groping for an explanation,
How would you counsel patients in a hurry?
Like Bell's palsy with unilateral lacrimation,
When, he is eating his meal of rice and curry.

The Physician believes it's due to degeneration,
Blames the greater superficial petrosal nerve,
But, is that the reason for this misconnection,
The lacrimal gland it was really meant to serve.

The Neurologist declares it is all due to excitation,
Sprouting from the lesser superficial petrosal nerve,
Involves the lacrimal gland which gets innervation,
When actually it is the parotid gland it should serve.

The Surgeon says he knows the correct operation,
Confidently tell the confused patient not to worry,
Cuts the tympanic branch of the IXth, best solution,
Lo and behold, no lacrimation eating rice and curry!

Background: It was customary for the medical staff at a rural mission hospital in South India to accept gifts in kind from patients, mostly home-grown fruits and vegetables, in order not to displease the simple and good-natured villagers! Once, a stool sample brought by a patient, wrapped in a banana leaf and meant for the laboratory was mistakenly taken home by an elderly doctor assuming it to be a personal gift!

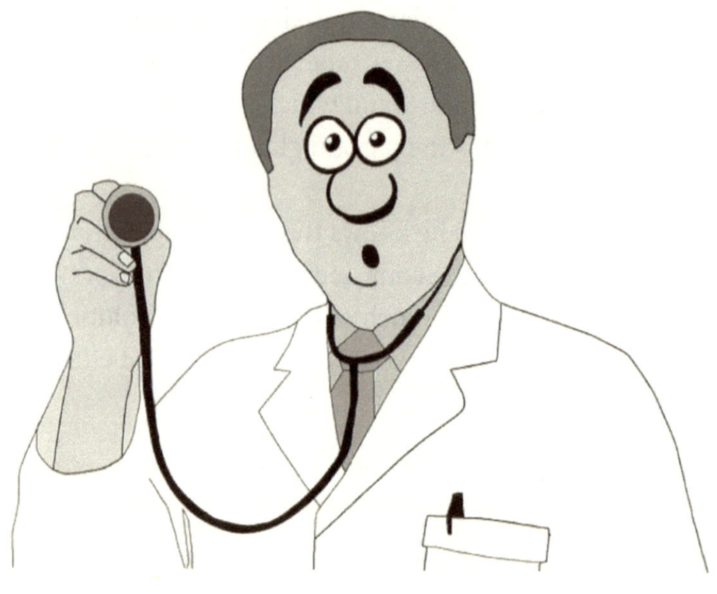

(Source: Pixabay)

TIME TO RETIRE

The villagers simply adored him for years,
Instantly he would diagnose their problems,
Momentarily, now appeared a bit inattentive,
Even his impaired hearing went unnoticed!
They loved his pleasant talk and gentle ways.
Of late, he failed to identify cases, old or new!
Regular fees, from the poor, he never insisted.
Even fruits or vegetables were shyly accepted.
Till the day his wife found that stinking object.
Instead of going to the lab came to her kitchen,
Realizing that his senses were failing one by one,
Eventually, the good old doctor agreed to retire!

NB: This is an example of an acrostic poem which spells out the title of the poem itself.

HAPPY BIRTHDAY!

(Dedicated to all my dear classmates)

Greeting comes once a year,
Without fail, you'll also hear,
May God give you, 'long life',
Aware, old age trials are rife!

Aging comes with a package,
Few can handle that baggage,
What if you aren't able player?
'Long life', a wish, not a prayer!

Can one forget low back ache?
Or slouching gait and no brake?
Why urgency confounds belief,
For frequent trips to find relief?

Recollect anecdotes of the past,
Fails to recall what one ate last!
Names sound, at times, strange,
Have faces undergone a change?

God gifted us a body, do take care,
Put on your walking shoes to dare,
Your friends for a stroll in the park,
Soon you will see in them, a spark!

A balanced diet, light & moderate,
To decide your structure & weight,
Just as, early to bed & early to rise,
Turns you healthy, wealthy & wise!

Show them how to age with grace,
Erase the wrinkles without a trace!
Attention! All ye Septuagenarians,
Ready to march as Octogenarians?

Background: There is an obsession among most people to get a "quick cure" and many are willing to pay a fortune for that. The pharmaceutical industry on one hand and the protagonists of traditional therapies on the other hand, exploit this craze by marketing their products with attractive video clips and posters using famous stars and sportspersons.

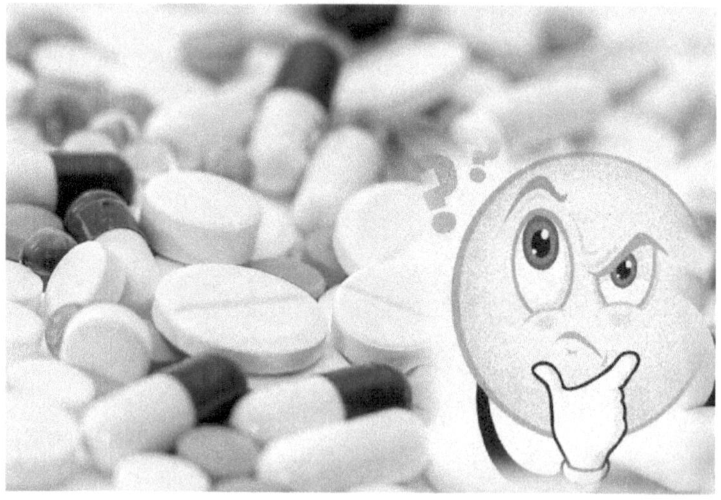

(Source: Pixabay)

The poem highlights the fact that God has bestowed a built-in system within all of us which many are not aware. There is a need to promote regular exercise and proper nutrition and highlight the risks associated with tobacco use and alcohol abuse. There is truth in the adage, "don't simply add years to life, but add life to years"!

DOSE FOR HAPPINESS

'**D**' is for that hormone called Dopamine,
A 'feel-good' factor that's released inside,
When words of praise smell like jasmine,
Each time one works with passion untied!

Hugs from kith or kin are beyond measure,
Such welcome actions end in a warm gush.
'**O**' is for Oxytocin that guarantees pleasure,
Though intimate gestures make some blush!

When the desire to help others truly exceeds,
Through timely services and acts of devotion,
'**S**' is for Serotonin, flows from positive deeds,
And quickly unlocks the floodgates of emotion!

Whether on a treadmill or out in jogger's park,
'**E**' is for Endorphins, comes handy when lost,
Elevates your mood or lights up when it's dark,
DOSE is God's remedy for happiness at no cost?

Background: In his book, 'Defeat into Victory', General William Slim wrote about the high malaria rates (>70%) among his soldiers because they refused to take the "foul-tasting" mepacrine. He said "Good doctors are no use without good discipline; more than half the battle against the disease is fought not by doctors but by the regimental officers". Malaria treatment was strictly enforced and the rate came down (<5%). It is said that the physical and mental turnaround in the army under him was a contributory factor to the eventual defeat of the Japanese in Burma.

NB: The curious incident of "Sun down, sleeves down," was described by the poet's father, Lt. Col. Kirti Jayavanth Raju (inset), who as a young Captain in the Indian Army Medical Corps, served as a Regimental Medical Officer (RMO) with the 14th Army in Burma.

FRIENDLY FIRE!

In the year nineteen hundred and forty-four,
The 14th Army under General William Slim,
With British and Indian soldiers in the core,
Were fully armed to win the battle for him.

But as they marched on it became very clear,
The deep jungles of Burma had more in store,
Not the enemy but dreaded mosquitoes to fear,
The count from malaria rapidly became more.

An order was issued to control the situation,
'Sun-down, sleeves down' was only other way,
With vigilance enforced to ensure prevention.
So, the battle-ready RMO finally had his say.

He shouted 'Sleeves down', at an errant one,
To discover the General to his utter disbelief,
Who complied with a grin, "Doc, well done,"
Only then, the RMO sighed with great relief!

Background: The Moringa Tree's value has been recognized by the United Nations Food and Agriculture Organization. Since ages, the nutritional value of the leaves, drumsticks and seeds and its healing property have been studied and used for many ailments and conditions. In Ayurvedic medicine, it is reported to cure as many as 300 diseases. It is one of the fastest selling "super foods" in the western world.

Source: SC

THE TREE OF LIFE

In my grandma's garden there is a big tree,
With green leaves, drumsticks and flowers,
Drumsticks in *sambar*, fried leaves in *ghee*,
Eaten with steamed rice for magic powers!

Among all the trees, the Moringa is unique,
Known in Asia, Africa and even in the west,
All parts of the tree good for one's physique,
Even the bark, seeds, roots passed the test!

Filled with vitamins, amino acids and protein,
Antioxidants, minerals from leaves and seeds,
More than milk, yogurt, carrots in your cuisine,
And much iron to fulfill all your dietary needs!

Economic value of the tree covers wide range,
From food, medicines, biofuel to animal feed,
Revegetation to mitigation of climate change,
Just a Tree of Life or a Miracle Tree indeed!

Background: A poignant reminder that doctors cannot perform miracles and when the time is up, death gently takes over.

SILENT TRUCE

As I stared down the dimly lit sanitized corridor,
Somewhere, a trolley squeaked, a door banged,
Swiftly muffling the voices from the general ward,
Slowly, I sneaked to the corner bed with curtains.

She lay motionless under a spotless white sheet,
Without any trace of distress etched on her face,
Perhaps floating in a post-operative unreal world,
Standing beside her, I pondered what I would say.

Would she ever know the advanced stage inside?
Or, that it was a simply an "open and shut" case,
Abruptly, as though she had sensed my presence,
Her eyes opened, the eloquent gaze unnerved me.

With great effort, I marshaled my counseling skills,
A welcome smile flickered across her serene face,
In that moment, I felt a warning not to say anything,
Our eyes were locked; for a moment, time stood still!

No words were exchanged, only her eyes spoke,
When she didn't blink a second time and her smile,
Remained frozen forever, there was nothing to say,
She had gallantly signed her peace with her Maker!

Section-E: Innocently Impish

- The Taj Mahal
- A Tribute to Our Seniors
- Is life a game of cricket?
- Indians, Indians Everywhere
- Are Birds Better Than Us?
- Who Shall be the King?
- Names Don't Matter in Cricket
- Safe in the Cloud
- Do Names Matter?

Background: The poet vividly recollects the city-tour in Dublin with a group of international tourists, when the driver/guide, suddenly stopped the bus at an intersection. He then pointed to a restaurant and asked, "Why is the most famous monument of India, named after Dublin's popular restaurant?" The Irish humor let loose a cacophony of laughter as the tourists saw the sign board 'Taj Mahal'. The poet felt embarrassed as all eyes were on him, but that inspired him to write this poem!

Source: ACK

THE TAJ MAHAL

I was once asked cheekily by an Irish bloke,
Why one of India's most famous monument,
It was mischievously meant to be a local joke,
Was named after Dublin's popular restaurant?

I actually sniggered at his feigned ignorance,
A Mughal Emperor's love for his dear consort,
Turned a grave into an icon for remembrance,
Not a *tandoori* restaurant in each tourist resort!

Surely Taj Mahal is India's architectural wonder,
The name invokes something undeniably grand,
Globally exploited for its exceptional splendor,
From tea-bags to T-shirts, truly a famous brand!

If somebody had predicted three centuries ago,
The Emperor would've signed a royal deterrent,
To obstruct Taj being used as a commercial logo,
And established the very first worldwide patent!

Background: It has been a long annual tradition in colleges for senior students to welcome "freshers" through an initiation ceremony called "ragging". The rituals were usually within moderate limits of decency, but occasionally escalated to levels of mental trauma for some students. Currently, this practice is looked down by the administration and banned on paper but exists silently in spirit!

A TRIBUTE TO OUR SENIORS

When guys from best schools
Were swiftly dubbed as fools
We learnt the very first night
That, seniors are always right!

The college anthem set the pace
Correctly said, won their grace
Twisted lyrics of wicked seniors
Still with us even after 50 years!

For annual rituals held so dear
The sadistic pleasure was clear
Surely they had strange power
That made all 'freshers' to cower.

With queries that defied sanity
They stripped off our modesty
Rewinding our own conception
To a weird theory of evolution!

While some taunted in Hinglish
Others had pranks very devilish
As the timid silently shed tears
The brave concealed their fears!

Those less evil had silly notions
Sending us to rare destinations
Like climbing the closet to Shimla
Or going under the cot to Kerala!

The kind-hearted felt cleanliness
Could bribe the way to godliness
So the chosen ones with brooms
Were ordered to clean the rooms!

Truly, it was an extraordinary place
Year later with a smirk on each face
We greeted new unsuspecting lads
Dumped by their moms and dads!

The joyful innocence of schooldays
Replaced with new ideas and ways
Followed the initiation rites at night
Proof that seniors are always right!

Background: Cricket is a game that is supposed to have originated in England more than 500 years ago. However, it has become almost like a religion with faithful followers in many countries that are not part of the Commonwealth. The poet discovers an analogy between life and the game of cricket.

(Source: Pixabay)

IS LIFE A GAME OF CRICKET?

Does journey of life mirror the game of cricket?
Both are struggles for survival and supremacy,
Achieved by polishing of skills to save a wicket,
At the very feet of the Master to realize ecstasy.

The first innings tests the scope of preparation,
When you enter the arena with a partner in tow,
Amidst applause you take stock of the situation,
Radiating with confidence to face the mighty foe.

Thunderbolts scream past your ears in rapid fire,
You duck in time to stay alive from misadventure,
A cordon of opponents awaits the mistimed skier,
Your partner ambles for a mid-pitch timely lecture.

With caution and passion, you build a partnership,
Courting dame luck to reach the golden milestone,
Or even beyond expectation despite any hardship,
Soon home and abroad you're no longer unknown.

But the second innings is a different game of thrills,
As unpredictable weather Gods appear to threaten,
Nasty pitch too, plots to expose your lethargic skills,
Then survival instincts wheel you thru a new lesson.

Followers lookout with bated breath and silent prayer,
Patiently from the bat, a gasping single off a trajectory,
Even God from above marvels at this amazing player,
As drum-beats and trumpets herald the magic century!

Even the opponents congratulate you for playing well,
You excel in your final match, having given your word,
Suddenly, the next deadly delivery breaches the citadel,
A gentleman in white coat points a finger heavenward!

Background: This poem was inspired by a real-life encounter between an Indian doctor (visiting the US for the first time) and an inquisitive American kid. His advice to his friends who planned to follow later was, "Never say, I am an Indian in the US, lest you be mistaken for a Red Indian"!

(Source: Pixabay)

INDIANS, INDIANS EVERYWHERE

In Boston long ago, a kid queried my nationality,
Tourists do have funny anecdotes in their sack,
"I am an Indian", I replied posing like a celebrity,
"Then, where are your feathers", he shot back?

I clarified, "Red Indians with feathers in America,
Have no blood relations in a country called India,
Unlike those Indians who migrated to East Africa",
Wonder why such revelations aren't in the media?

Today, the Indian diaspora is scattered wide and far,
Covering the entire United Kingdom, USA, Canada,
From Bahrain to the Emirates, from Kuwait to Qatar,
Including small nations like Suriname and Grenada.

Surely, Indians are in Fiji, Mauritius and Malaysia,
Brought by colonial rulers to thrive in a new land,
To Sri Lanka and even to Réunion and Indonesia,
Few even migrated to Australia and New Zealand.

In Guyana, Trinidad, Tobago, rest of the Caribbean,
Folks recall their ancestors, who sailed from the East,
Even those Indians who call themselves Singaporean,
Still have their roots in parts of India, to say the least.

Indians go anywhere, even to places none will dare,
Migration today makes hodge-podge of civilization,
Seventeen million migrants from India everywhere,
Would "Made in India" lead to rapid globalization?

Background: Absolutely fascinated by the beauty and behavior of birds, in many countries, particularly in Asia and Africa, the poet has captured the uncanny comparison with human beings.

(Source of photos - Pixabay)

ARE BIRDS BETTER THAN US?

Birds are beautiful; they are not made like us,
Listen to African Catbirds singing in a forest,
Can sing and dance, even make a lot of fuss,
Would our finest singers be ready for a test?

Birds are beautiful; they are not made like us,
Black-winged Lovebirds truly are an inspiration,
Can sing and dance, even make a lot of fuss,
Could teach the dancing stars of our generation!

Birds are beautiful; they are not made like us,
Watch Thick-billed Ravens in an aerial display,
Can sing and dance, even make a lot of fuss,
They make sky-divers look like models of clay!

Birds are beautiful; they are not made like us,
Banded Barbets hang on trees upside down,
Can sing and dance, even make a lot of fuss,
Like in a circus, more amusing than a clown!

Birds are beautiful; they are not made like us,
But the White-collared Pigeon is a bit strange,
Can sing and dance, even make a lot of fuss,
Prefers to nest in a church or within the range!

Birds are beautiful, but why some are like us?
Note the Yellow-fronted Parrot, unlike the rest,
Few sing and dance, others make a lot of fuss,
Makes unmusical whistles like a squeaky pest!

Birds are beautiful, but why some are like us?
The calls of Forest Orioles are slurred together,
Few sing and dance; others make a lot of fuss,
Like several drunkards talking to one another!

Birds are beautiful, but why some are like us?
Follow the Spot-breasted Plover with the gait,
Few sing and dance; some make a lot of fuss,
Awkwardly like patients with Parkinson's fate!

• • •

(Source: Pixabay)

WHO SHALL BE THE KING?

Never before had there been an assembly,
On such a scale, all exotic and enchanting,
The air was tense, but not that unfriendly,
Despite sweet and sour feelings, exciting.

Sticking to tradition the Mango moved first,
"I am your King, let us begin without fear",
"You can't be King?" was the mad outburst,
"You are only seen some months in a year'!

The Apple cried, "Why am I always left out,
Even a child knows I keep the doctor away",
A Banana grunted, "Champs, without doubt,
Believe in me and take bites when they play".

The Avocado pooh-poohed it as rather trivial,
Factually it is known to be extra nutrient-rich,
With fat for energy more than a bowl of cereal,
Amazing culinary uses, no need for sales pitch.

One of the Cherries joined the condemnation,
"Haven't you heard the saying Cherry on top?"
The Durian at once smelt some discrimination,
Realized it was better to remain in the backdrop.

One of the dried Dates from the oil-rich desert,
Stated, "Available 365 days, any shop or mall",
The Fig hid his gut feelings, being an introvert,
Aware health benefits are known to one and all.

A red Grape quipped not to sound like a puppet,
"Proud as wine at royal banquets in every toast",
The Guava didn't want to blow his own trumpet,
Loaded with nutrients, sensed no need to boast!

Sitting separately, the Jackfruit was left to ponder,
If it's size that mattered, he would stake his claim,
The syndicate of Oranges didn't want to squander,
Their chances based on global popularity and fame.

The Papaya was reluctant to proclaim its genealogy,
Yet, ripe or raw widely popular in most Asian meals,
The Peaches and Pears shared a powerhouse analogy,
Both packed with vitamins and minerals for all deals.

The Pineapple already in a jam desired reassessment,
The Plums were well into diary and bakery business,
Were interested in the expansion of their investment,
Like the Pomegranates, given their taste for richness.

The Strawberry came as a spectator quite reluctantly,
Angry with botanists for the "false fruit" suggestion,
Is the Watermelon a vegetable some asked wantonly?
Others too came hopefully to settle their contention.

With regal acumen inherited from many generations,
The Mango declared "No need to go into depression,
Group action will be taken to meet your expectations,
However, it is time now to close this virtual session"!

Background: George Bernard Shaw once stated, "Cricket is a game of chance played by 11 fools against 11 fools and watched by 11,000 fools"!

NAMES DON'T MATTER IN CRICKET

Cricket once christened as a gentlemen's game,
Never stopped others who wished to seek fame,
Like a Loader, a Smith, a Butler or even a Cook,
Provided they knew cricket, to play by the book!

WG Grace, doctor & famed cricketer of his age,
His beard, bulk & batsmanship held centre stage,
Between bat and ball, and from wicket to wicket,
Many hail him as the inventor of modern cricket!

Gathering speed as if in a hundred-meter dash,
Pacers had guts to chuck the cherry to thrash,
Some were actually Stones, like Olly and Small,
But, the actions of Onions were enough to gall!

Once a bouncer from Cork hit a batsman's eye,
Like letting a cork from a champagne bottle fly,
Among the fastest pace bowlers, was a Wood,
Fancy a medium pacer, like Tongue to be good!

Doug Insole made his footprint as a cricketer,
Better known as a controversial administrator,
From Yorkshire came Boycott, batter supreme,
He made 246 not out; was left out of the team!

Nick, an opener, never became a real Knight,
But, Joe Root quit captaincy when it was right,
Grabbed a MBE & still dominates with the bat,
But Stokes proved he can play in any format!

Collingwood, in the slips, excelled in catches,
All the cricketers know catches win matches,
Among wicket keepers, best was Alan Knott,
Yes, for record dismissals; for stumpings not!

Amazingly, the Sidebottoms, father and son,
Both played test cricket; the father, just one,
Simon Brown too, was an "one-test wonder",
But Rory Burns in the Ashes didn't go under!

Long ago, WI pacers did Close, black & blue,
They wanted his wicket but he offered no clue,
Taking test hat-trick is many a bowler's dream,
From Bates to Broad, 14 for the English team!

Against India at Lords, strange to see a Pope,
Making his test debut, blest with luck & hope,
Succeeded to score 28 runs in his only knock,
But against Ireland, got 200 to swell his stock!

SAFE IN THE CLOUD?

One day, I gazed at the blue sky,
Mused if God has Plan-B in mind,
When He made clouds to float by,
Warm & Cold, two forms of a kind!

Lately, my grandson during a break,
Stayed with me and bridged the gap,
Shared photos; some real, few fake,
Of places and pals stored on an App.

Hundreds of photos safe in a Cloud,
And other devices of his generation,
He enlightened me and I felt proud,
Getting wiser to digital configuration!

I reminisced when as a ten-year old,
Vacationing at my grandpa's home,
I could not suppress becoming bold,
To clamber up and check the dome.

Poised on a ladder shaky & cracked,
I surveyed the ugly cobwebs of time,
Hiding few boxes taped and stacked,
Unclear if my snooping was a crime.

Nonetheless, attempted to open one,
Triggered by a tantalizing obsession,
Keepsakes ne'er exposed to the sun,
Now clearly visible in my possession!

Albums with photos, black and white,
Few moth-eaten, some faded & torn,
Mementos of days, beautiful & bright,
Of a bygone generation, left to mourn.

Imagine if folks like grandpa preferred,
To store photos and papers in iCloud,
What if they forgot to share password?
Access to accounts will not be allowed!

Background: Salem is an industrial town in Tamil Nadu. Wenlock Downs is a rolling meadow in Ooty, a hill station. Toponymy describes how Hamilton Bridge named after its builder became Barber's Bridge. The natives found it difficult to say Hamilton and started calling it Ambaton! (*Ambaton* in Tamil, means barber)! Ironically, the bridge was renamed Barber's Bridge!

DO NAMES MATTER?

People do debate as if names really matter,
With regime change, always there's chatter,
So what, if in UK & USA, there's Manchester,
Or a Salem in India, & 36 in USA, any better?

The British turned hill stations into resorts,
For those rich and for travelers of all sorts,
With English & Scottish names that beckon,
Like Wenlock Downs, a meadow to reckon!

Talli enjoyed the sobriquet 'Little England',
The colonial rulers obsessed of motherland,
Was it fair weather, or the rural landscape,
Or specially to find a quiet place to escape?

But, with Hamilton Bridge, all went wrong,
Locals called it *Ambaton Bidge* before long,
Barbers are referred to by that Tamil name,
So now it's Barber's Bridge, whom to blame?

Section-F: Philosophically Provocative

- The Wheel of Fashion
- The Return of the Catamarans
- Where is Hope for the Hopeless?
- Grandpa's Magic Words
- Forgotten Forever
- There is a Song in Every Heart
- Till We Meet Again
- A Septuagenarian's Wish
- No Time to Say Goodbye
- My Treasure Island
- A Four-Letter Word
- The Rickshaw Man
- I am a Cuckoo Bird
- The Art and Craft of Survival
- True or False?
- Confessions of an Old-timer

Background: The "wheel of fashion" has made a full circle since the days of Adam and Eve. Today's generation have discarded flowing robes and long gowns and adopted scanty outfits, see-through dresses and tattered jeans! Not long ago, people in tattered clothes were looked down as being the poorest of the poor who could not afford decent clothes. We consider aborigine tribes backward and want them to be educated and wear clothes to appear civilized!

(Source: Pixabay)

THE WHEEL OF FASHION

When God created the Garden of Eden,
Innocence and nudity meant the same,
Till the day the forbidden fruit was eaten,
Led to fig-leaves, sheepskin and shame.

When humans finally invented the wheel,
It ushered an era of fortune and fashion,
Fabrics of silk, wool and cotton a new deal,
For the affluent became their only passion.

Shattered and tattered, the poor stay bare,
Helpless to hide their modesty or ancestry,
The rich in flowing robes and yards to spare,
Strut without shame in pomp and pageantry.

But today, for the sirens of the silver screen,
Sex appeal is the name of the modern game,
Like mannequins on the catwalk set to preen,
The more one reveals the higher one's fame.

Human anatomy has a unique mystique still,
Males and females compete with one another,
Exposing their nudity for profit, or just for thrill,
Like nudist camps where families are together.

Even today in deep jungles roam naked tribes,
Wearing only beads, whatever be their motive,
Are they God's own people with guiltless vibes,
Or by our civilized standards, most primitive?

Background: Traditionally, the fishermen in coastal Tamil Nadu, use catamarans for their fishing forays into the Bay of Bengal. The word catamaran is derived from the Tamil word "kattu" meaning tie and "maran" for wood. Dangerous though it may seem, these intrepid fishermen for generations, have been able to supply fish to the local market. Despite the fact that they have to compete with the mechanized fishing trawlers and face many problems at sea including natural hazards, nothing will deter their daily dalliance with destiny.

THE RETURN OF THE CATAMARANS

Anxious women squat on the sultry beach,
Scanning the skyline with their naked eyes,
With suckling babies crawling within reach,
Lost in prayer, as giant waves roll and rise.

Not a sextant or a compass to guide their way,
Gambling with life is the fishermen's profession,
While their experience is from the sea each day,
They want their children to have good education.

But for the wealthy tourists from different lands,
Those on catamarans are just stupid not brave,
Visitors who come for fun and frolic on the sands,
Don't care if one fisherman meets a watery grave.

Black specks over the horizon break the tension,
Soon catamarans come slicing through the waves,
Now the tourists with cameras are ready for action,
To click the reunion of the wives and their braves!

Background: We hear of horrendous stories of new-born babies being found near public dustbins every day from cities all over the world. The dedication and compassion shown by the Sisters of the Missionaries of Charity (MOC) while taking care of abandoned babies and orphan children, is truly amazing.

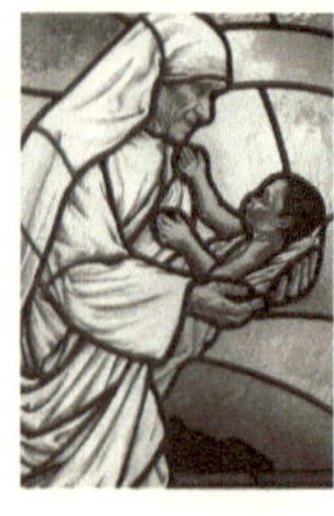

"In some countries there is no hunger for bread. But people are suffering from terrible loneliness, terrible despair, terrible hatred, feeling unwanted, helpless and hopeless. They have forgotten how to smile; they have forgotten the beauty of the human touch. They are forgetting what human love is"

– Mother Teresa

WHERE IS HOPE FOR THE HOPELESS?

A stray mongrel, sniffing leftovers,
Startled by whimper from the trash,
Alerts those hurrying off,
Homeless soul bends to see,
Finds newborn alive,
Picks up with love,
Has no roof,
Cash or
Food.

NB: This is a nine-line poem called Nonet. The first line has nine syllables; the next line has eight syllables and so on; the last line has just one syllable.

Background: The poet spent his early childhood with his grandparents in Madras. His grandfather, Rev. Gopalaswamy would take him to the Marina beach often. It served the mutual interests of both; his grandfather found place to meditate and the grandson got a play area with plenty of sand and water!

MY GRANDPA'S MAGIC WORDS

Sitting cross-legged on the warm sand,
My grandpa was soon lost in meditation,
Stroking his beard, away in another land,
While I played alone with my imagination.

Tiny handfuls of sand to build a mountain,
Then pushing my favorite red sports car,
Up to the top to a make-believe fountain,
Then speeding down like a shooting star.

When it was time to go I searched around,
Grandpa knew at once without being told,
My favorite sports car was not to be found,
He saw inside the mind of a three-year old.

'Don't worry, we'll get another one", he said,
Whenever in trouble I still remember to say,
What he taught me that day to move ahead,
'I am getting better day by day in every way'!

(Source: Pixabay)

FORGOTTEN FOREVER

Avaricious political rulers and selected royalty,
Beautifully sculptured in granite for perpetuity,
Chosen as superhuman legends for inspiration,
Despite being oppressors known for corruption,
Even ostentatiously documented in school books.
Far above honest teachers as if they are crooks,
Generally extolled for their academic dedication,
Humbly accepting teaching as their life's ambition,
Indeed, their noble efforts to mould future citizens,
Jestingly compared as labor of ordinary denizens.
Known for their sex appeal, film stars do acts lewd,
Leave nothing to the imagination and appear nude,
Money and fame spreads their name far and wide,
None would be forgotten; except those with pride,
Offering their knowledge and services to the society,
Professionals- nurses, midwives, rest of the fraternity,
Quickly respond, ambulance drivers and fire-fighters,
Rescue victims from the jaws of death, inspire writers
Script their valiant efforts lest folks forget their deeds.
Trampled in the dust are farmers, who toil in the fields,
Unsung heroes who provide sources for sustenance,
Volunteers, who assist during pandemic or pestilence,
Workers in risky vocations like coal mines ill-managed,
X-rays would reveal their lungs being seriously ravaged,
Youthfulness sacrificed for family survival sans sympathy,
Zeal for work deserves appreciation and entails empathy!

Background: Composed as a song for the beatification ceremony of Mother Teresa in Phnom Penh, Cambodia, 2003.

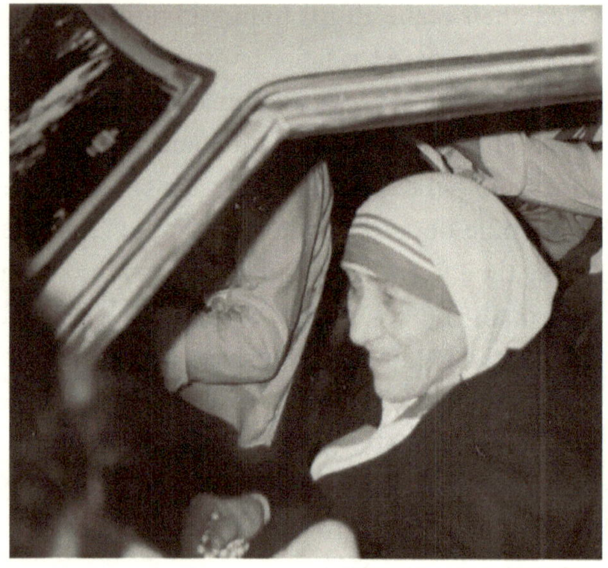

Source: DJ

THERE IS A SONG IN EVERY HEART

Truly, there is a song in every heart,
And a heart that sings in every person,
Bring out the drums, strum the guitars,
Since life is music and music is love.

There is much chaos in every country,
Yet, in each nation there's always hope,
De-mine the land and destroy weapons,
Since peace is life and life is precious.

Lifestyle of the rich is ruined by wealth,
Poor turn poorer seeking good health,
Burn your selfishness, bury your greed,
Caring for the poor means serving God.

Truly, there is a song in every heart,
And a heart that sings in every person,
So, build bridges with all less fortunate,
Compassion for others is more precious!

Background: The poet had developed close friendship with people from diverse cultures and ethnic background, having travelled far and wide and worked in many countries. Bidding farewell to friends whom he may never see again was one of the most emotional moments he ever experienced in his life.

(Source: Pixabay)

TILL WE MEET AGAIN

Wishing farewell in any language,
As you may never meet tomorrow,
Not so easy for people of any age.
Parting always has a bit of sorrow.

Dosvidaniya in Russian is the same,
Auf Wiedersehen bit too hard to say,
Unlike *Sayonara,* more like a game,
Non-Germans actually feel that way.

For young people in Europe it's *Ciao,*
400 million will say *Adios* in Spanish,
Goodbye rhymes with Chinese *chow,*
Similarly, *Żegnaj* is sendoff in Polish.

Arrivederci is goodbye for the Italian,
For the French it is *Au revoir* for bye,
Like *Adeus* spoken by the Brazilian,
Wrongly said can make matters wry!

Namaste is for welcome and farewell,
Goodbye in Malay, like *Selamat jalan,*
Makes it easy for non-Indians as well,
In Mandarin, pronounce it as *Zài jiàn!*

Khuda hafiz when parting is in Persian,
Or *Ma'a as-salaama* in the Middle East,
The equivalent is *Annyeong* in Korean,
Not easy for those who speak it least!

Sure friendship binds strangers together,
There is heaviness in the hearts to bear,
When one has to say farewell to another,
That's why plan for good times to share!

A SEPTUAGENARIAN'S WISH

Let me just take what is mine,
Accolades of public adoration,
All that was free, fair and fine,
Some in awe and admiration!

Let the appreciation I earned,
Not be seen in kind or wealth,
Or penned to be later burned,
Rather, alive in public health!

Let that remain till end of time,
Within the cluster like folklore,
Stimulate others in their prime,
Prick the ego of all who bore!

Let me hence take what's mine,
Fragrant memories of affection,
From generations down the line,
To rest in peace after separation!

NO TIME TO SAY GOODBYE

A final gasp, a few heart-beats later,
The one we loved just left our midst,
There was no time to say goodbye,
Or we'll meet again in another world.

Most people do agree death is cruel,
When it snatches one, young in years,
So is there really a life beyond death,
Or such thoughts just to keep us alive?

Is there somewhere a heavenly abode?
A place where the good are rewarded,
A promised land of eternal peace and joy,
Where ultimately we all shall meet again?

But this I know, life shall not be the same,
Though your unseen presence is felt here,
Would anguish and sorrow vanish with time,
Or sweet memories, a balm to heal our scars?

Background: This poem in acrostic format describes the feelings of a young woman who was devastated by the sudden demise of her husband and her one-year old baby in quick succession.

MY TREASURE ISLAND

Moments after the sun has vanished,
Yonder into the depths of the ocean,
The day's work comes to a standstill,
Return to my room with weary steps,
Enticed by a strange sense of longing,
All around is a stony wall of silence,
Solitude once again grips my thoughts,
Ushering a sense of helpless impatience,
Remembering the loss of kith and kin,
Events filled with queries of "Why me"?
Instill a purpose in life to find answers,
Slumber pulls the shutters of my eyes,
Lifts me to a fascinating domain of joy,
Above the clouds, to a world of dreams,
Near and dear ones embrace me tightly,
Dreams unite us all in my treasure island!

Background: Globally, predicting the future is big-time business for many. People, from aristocrats to the ordinary, wish to know in advance what FATE has in store for them. Only some believe that God has a PLAN for each person.

A FOUR-LETTER WORD

Since ancient times, the planets and stars,
Have trapped innocent humans in fantasy,
From birth through life the effect of Mars,
Appeared to rule one's Fate despite fallacy.

Astronomers revealed the cosmic landscape,
Despite variances from Ptolemy to Galileo,
Astrologers design dubious means to escape,
For zodiac followers from Sagittarius to Leo!

When vicissitudes in life ruin one's affluence,
Astrologers will claim that it's all due to Fate,
Thus attribute to new planetary malevolence,
But rationalists say it doesn't hold any weight.

Some consider Fate is preset by sins of the past,
Others curse Fate for suffering in one's lifespan,
Few alter lifestyles; aware good times don't last,
Only true believers are certain God has a PLAN!

Background: Since the end of the 19th century, one of the oldest and most 'cruel' means of transport for short distances in India, were hand-pulled rickshaws. The rickshaw pullers were generally poor and uneducated and were forced to accept this work even though it provided a meagre source of livelihood for their families.

Source: RVR

THE RICKSHAW-MAN

The rickshaw-man interrupts his run,
Merely to pause for a hurried lunch,
Beneath the sweltering midday sun,
Cold rice with raw chilies to munch.

Barefoot along the city's thoroughfare,
Heedless of painful blisters on his feet,
From dawn to dusk he pulls with care,
Avoiding rest to make both ends meet.

Born in poverty, never went to school,
Nobody taught him to multiply or divide,
But don't imagine he's an absolute fool,
Learned to add and subtract with pride.

His only ambition in life is to set aside,
All income for his family in the village,
Where a lack of vaccines left his child,
Differently-abled at a very young age.

Background: The analogy between a man-made clock using a cuckoo bird and a real cuckoo bird enjoying its existence in nature where "all things are bright and beautiful", ends with the distinct "koo-kooo" sounds made by both. The rest is obvious.

(Source: Pixabay)

I AM A CUCKOO BIRD

I'm a Cuckoo bird dainty and small,
From the nation of clocks faraway,
I have my pride of place on the wall,
And don't stop singing night or day!

My 'koo-kooo' kept everyone on time,
Elders to office, the kids off to school,
Family and neighbors trust my chime,
Even in Winter I don't lose my cool!

One Spring morning, a familiar sound,
Certainly didn't come from the phone,
Could there be a new Cuckoo around?
Or had someone else copied my tone?

Through a window I saw him on a tree,
A Cuckoo singing the beauty of nature,
A world where all are blissful and free,
God-made, only for an earthly creature!

Background: Human beings have learnt the skills of survival. While some are more resilient than others, it is still a big challenge for all. Generally, society is made up of people who are righteous and always struggling, those who are wicked and usually seen enjoying life, with the moderates sandwiched in between. No one can predict who should live up to a ripe old age! Is it due to one's *Karma*?

THE ART AND CRAFT OF SURVIVAL

Will a doctor who can't engineer a miracle cure.
Continue to ask his patient to be patient forever?
An engineer won't doctor his blueprint for sure.
To cause a dam to burst with no means to cover!

Honestly, washing machines make clothes fresh.
Exposing dirty linen in public is a tabloid's goal.
Maquillage of many a celeb ripped off the flesh.
Challenging lesser mortals to crawl out of a hole!

Does a preacher actually practice what he teaches,
To escape from a carefully planned sting operation?
Unless a wise teacher wastes little time on speeches,
But strives to lay a foundation for good education!

Are days on earth numbered with lifestyle we choose.
Should workers of iniquity go first with apprehension?
Followed by all the upright after the end of the cruise,
Or is there a weird Karma that defies comprehension?

Background: A *billet-doux* camouflaged as a Nonet (nine-line poem) with first line having nine syllables and successive lines having 8, 7, 6, 5, 4, 3, 2 and ending with 1 syllable.

TRUE OR FALSE?

When you smile your eyes sparkle with joy
I see happiness in your face
When the tears roll down your cheeks
Can feel your silent pain
I see my image
Like a mirror
In your eyes
Is this
Love?

CONFESSIONS OF AN OLD-TIMER

I dye my hair and say age is just a number,
Can't understand why I slip into a slumber,
Right in the middle of a grave conversation,
Letting folks think I am in deep meditation!

Hate hearing aids, even if virtually invisible,
Pretend can hear, know that's unforgivable,
When advice is sought on a topic or profile,
Though blissfully oblivious, a benign smile!

Thankfully sight is better after laser surgery,
Reading without glasses, no fear of perjury,
But no matter what, I can't dare to venture,
From my own bathroom minus my denture!

The timely triple by-pass, sustains my heart,
Therapeutic yoga keeps me upright & smart,
Hides my lordosis and ankylosing spondylitis,
Curious if acupuncture is worthy for arthritis!

Oh God, the time has come for my confession,
Though proud of the things in my possession,
I'm scared to lose one when I go out to roam,
What if I fail to recall in a park, where's home?

• • •

(Source: Pixabay)

SIGNIFICANCE OF A DASH

(*DoB – DoD*)

Every individual's lifespan on earth,
From the precise date of one's birth,
Till death finally reduces one to ash,
Is separated simply by a small dash!

At birth, all gather around the cradle,
The neonate is like a fairy in the fable,
Praises pour from friends & relatives,
Expectations surpass all superlatives!

Gradually, the kid is tutored at school,
May emerge a genius or remain a tool,
But, life is a roller-coaster for one & all,
Some earn laurels, many tumble & fall.

All the gravestones in every cemetery,
For civilians and those in the military,
Are rightly special for family to trace,
The departed soul's last resting place.

Engraved on a marble or any stone,
Some sanctified verses well-known,
For all to see, the deceased's name,
And also the person's deeds & fame.

The newspapers too print an obituary,
Notifying the death of some dignitary,
Even legends from films, sports & art,
May not be forgotten when they depart.

All who changed the world live forever,
History won't record normal folk, never,
But between births & deaths, only a **dash**,
Recaps our lives, before we turn into ash!

Section-G: Politically Persuaded

- A New World Order
- Air Raids and Beating Hearts
- Mirage in the Desert
- Fifty Years After Independence
- Malo Aupito, Dear Lord!
- Myth for the Masses
- Why is the World Divided?

Background: This was written during the time of the Gulf War (1991) when the poet worked with the Ministry of Health in Saudi Arabia. On 7 August 1990, Operation Desert Shield was signaled in response to Iraq's invasion of Kuwait to herald a "new world order". After the failure of talks between the Allied Forces and Iraq, Operation Desert Storm began on 17 January 1991.

(Source: Pixabay)

A NEW WORLD ORDER

Where peaceful Bedouin caravans,
Once roamed freely over the sands,
Today, battle-hungry armored vans,
And tanks rumble from other lands.

Where once birds engaged in migration,
Flapped across the sky as part of nature,
Today, combat jets in deadly formation,
Fly above fiercely as a war-time feature.

Where once cacophony of animal sounds,
And shrieking broke the desert eeriness,
Today, earsplitting heavy artillery rounds
Reverberate around in deathly stillness.

Where once sandstorms swirled sky-high,
As part of nature's fury and its ordinance,
Today, dark clouds rise as end draws nigh
Of burning oilfields amidst rival pursuance.

Where once plan- Operation Desert Shield
Was designed to pursue a new World Order,
Today, Operation Desert Storm would wield,
Massive firepower aimed beyond the border.

Background: During the first Gulf War (1991), it was reported that Iraqi scud missiles did land on Saudi soil and there were deaths and casualties too. The fear generated by the possibility that "weapons of mass destruction" might be used created more panic and anxiety among residents and expatriates living in the capital and other border areas.

(Source: Pixabay)

AIR RAIDS AND BEATING HEARTS

As sleep descends silently,
like a dense fog to envelope the city,
the young and old in homes and hotels
relax in beds of warm luxury,
Suddenly all-around screaming sirens
spear the Arabian tranquility.
Brutally shaken, men, women and children
listen to impending danger.
With beating hearts, they scramble
through a maze of chaos to safety,
The more cautious with gas masks,
the less fortunate with wet towels.
Earth-shattering sounds echo,
as they watch in horror and anxiety.
Different nationalities brought together,
bound by fear, united in hope.
As silent prayers escape from dry throats
for help from the Almighty.

Background: The never-ending peace process in the Middle East has not yielded the expected results despite global efforts. People on both sides want to stop the bloodshed and pray for harmony, amity and trust. Will they ever achieve their dreams or is it just a mirage in the desert?

(Source: Pixabay)

MIRAGE IN THE DESERT

Over burning sand dunes,
Through merciless desert storms,
Like their forefathers who taught them
how to face nature's fury,
The Bedouins with their goats and camels,
Trudge relentlessly against all odds

in their eternal search,
For the shimmering oasis of life,
far, far away in the distance.
When the heat of the day melts
into the cool darkness of night,
They would sink their weary limbs
Around hastily-built campfires,
As they feast and drink,
The young sing and dance with abandon,
The elders watch the sparkling stars
And the shape of the moon,
As it plays hide and seek like a virgin bride
Behind a veil of clouds.

Even before the golden rays of the sun
Can herald another dawn,
They prepare for a long and grueling journey
Into the unknown,
The battle for survival must continue
As it always has in the past,
While the crusade for peace
Shall ever remain an eternal struggle.
Will the footprints on the sands,
Lead to the mirage in the desert?

Background: This poem was originally written in July 1997, to commemorate the 50th anniversary of India's independence. It vividly sums up the challenges faced by the country and the progress made by the nation after throwing off the yoke of colonialism and building a foundation based on democracy.

FIFTY YEARS OF INDEPENDENCE

India's epic struggle for independence,
Helped to bring the Union Jack down,
Led by Gandhi's spirit of non-violence,
Raised the Tricolor in village and town.

Fifty years ago, many promises were made,
Nehru's dream of a nation secular and strong,
With unachieved targets turned hopes to fade,
And with successive governments went wrong.

Another Gandhi (Indira) earned her fame,
Displaced stalwarts of the era of liberation,
By transforming politics into a chess game,
And replaced them with a younger generation.

A famous capital for the Royalty in the past,
Delhi joined the cities with worst air pollution,
Soon awakened the environmentalists at last,
While exposing political scams and corruption.

Mother Teresa's mission of service and hope,
Where market economy coexists with Marxism,
Showed the poor of Calcutta the way to cope,
While elsewhere death bells toll for communism.

The Gateway of India still stands in Bombay,
Is Asia's largest slum at Dharavi just a legacy?
The symbol of colonialism in today's Mumbai,
Or proof of progress made under democracy?

Madras became Chennai with a stroke of the pen,
Setting the clock back while others silently resent,
The cultural renaissance in the hands of few men,
Making a melting pot of the past and the present.

Launching of Indian rockets into outer space,
To deter neighbors from unscrupulous deeds,
And followed by investments in the arms race,
Diverted resources reserved for basic needs.

But India is a perfect example of unity in diversity,
Where different faiths and sects are in abundance,
The people are known for their vigor and vitality,
Everyone firmly believes in the gospel of tolerance.

Family values, love and respect for elders still exists,
Social reforms have empowered the weaker society,
Old-age homes and meals-on-wheels no one insists,
Even the President is from a backward community.

The wheel of progress will take us into the 21st century,
With the pace of the industrial revolution, says the media,
Economists claim that our brains will enrich the treasury,
An Asian super-power built on democracy will be India.

So, after fifty long years of independence, we are proud,
All nations should ensure democratic values do not rust,
The "ballot" is superior to the "bullet", we proclaim aloud,
Universal peace shall only be achieved by mutual trust!

Background: *Malo Aupito*, Dear Lord was composed in August 2008 for the coronation celebrations in honor of King George V held in Nuku'alofa, Tonga. '*Malo Aupito*' means 'thank you' in Tongan. The lead singer was Suresh Jayavant, accompanied by Vaka Poleo and DJ Darren's band. https://www.youtube.com/watch?v=j6k6NFlQJm0

In 2009, this song was adapted and translated by Rev (Dr.) Siotame Havea into Tongan, as the theme song for the Health Promoting Churches Partnership, initiated by the author, when he led the WHO Country Liaison Office in Tonga. It was aimed to support the Ministry of Health to combat the threat from non-communicable diseases.

MALO AUPITO, DEAR LORD!

From the friendly islands of Tonga,
Where the sun rises first,
Mostly for us, later for the rest,
Living in different lands,
Malo, malo, malo, malo,
Malo aupito dear Lord!

From the royal capital of Tonga,
Where stands the Ha'amonga,
Of a nation, proud and strong,
With its own rich tradition
Malo, malo, malo, malo,
Malo aupito dear Lord!

From the scattered islands of Ha'apai,
Where people face nature's fury,
They conquered the daunting sea,
And survived, cyclones and storms,
Malo, malo, malo, malo,
Malo aupito dear Lord!

From the warm waters of Vava'u,
Where humpback whales from afar,
Like all God's creatures of the sea,
Come every year to mate,
Malo, malo, malo, malo,
Malo aupito dear Lord!

From the beautiful island of 'Eua,
Where virgin forests thrive,
And frigate birds, glide from cliffs,
Under the tropical rain,
Malo, malo, malo, malo,
Malo aupito dear Lord!

For the gifted people of Tonga,
Who preserved their art & culture,
With their singing and dancing,
Making mats and tapa,
Malo, malo, malo, malo,
Malo, aupito dear Lord!

To these friendly islands of Tonga,
Came missionaries from far and wide,
To preach the holy gospel and,
Prepare God's kingdom on earth,
Malo, malo, malo, malo,
Malo aupito dear Lord!

• • •

Background: Refers to the turmoil in some countries which led to violence and regime change, after the war in Iraq.

MYTH FOR THE MASSES

Ancient cities illuminated in flames,
Like giant funeral pyres in the desert,
Old regimes washed away in blood,
Of innocent screams and bold fists.

Get liberty, equality and fraternity,
That is what the leaders preached,
And the poor masses lived in belief,
And toiled like slaves for generations.

They built palaces for their rulers,
So that their huts would be safe,
They killed offenders of the regime,
So, their children get milk and honey.

Let not grief dismantle your sanity,
Nor revenge lead to destruction,
Who knows the price of freedom
To escape the hangman's noose?

Priceless treasures have been plundered,
Good governance sits on worthless paper,
While corrupt politicians enjoy the throne,
Democracy remains a myth for the masses!

(Source: Pixabay)

WHY IS THE WORLD DIVIDED?

Since the dawn of civilization,
Disputes ended in bloodshed,
The price paid for domination,
And continued by rulers misled.

Why the world remains divided,
On race or color, caste or creed,
Innocents crushed, left for dead,
Aren't dogs proud of their breed?

Today, civil wars destroy society,
Chasing meek refugees on the run,
Gone is liberty, equality, fraternity,
To die in no-man's land in the sun.

Why all nations remain alienated,
On progress and quest for peace,
Or stop a nation being devastated,
To ensure democracy a fresh lease?

Section-H: Deadly Disasters

- Dead Birds and Broken Wings
- The Great Earthquake
- Wrath of God or Global Warming
- Wild Fires
- The Invisible Machine
- Animal Propensities of Mankind

Background: Bangladesh is one of the countries that has repeatedly borne the brunt of cyclones and storms and the people living in coastal areas have suffered enormously. This was written in 1985 to highlight the agony and grief of the people of Bangladesh when a severe cyclone with a wind speed of 154 km per hour and 3.0 to 4.6 storm surge killed more than 11,000 people and destroyed more than 94,000 homes.

DEAD BIRDS AND BROKEN WINGS

Weather pundits and satellite pictures
Give warning of nature's imminent rage
Mostly for people in concrete structures
Fully insured against death or damage.

Who cares for the poor bird in the tree
Perched high in a fragile nest of its own
Could have gone anywhere, it was free
Instead of foolishly waiting to be blown.

Hail stones, lightning and thunder
Break some panes and strike fast
Folks dismiss it as nature's blunder
To attack buildings designed to last.

Gale-force winds with revengeful pace
Threaten the birds and eggs in the nest
Was it meant to destroy the whole race
Or simply put hundreds of birds to rest?

Background: The famous 9-storey Dharahara Tower in Kathmandu partially survived an earthquake in 1834, but was severely damaged by another earthquake in 1934. It was rebuilt but was reduced to rubble by the massive earthquake that hit Nepal on 25 April 2015. More than 600,000 other buildings that included historic and ancient structures, temples and homes of ordinary people were also damaged or destroyed. More than 9,000 people lost their lives and thousands were injured. (Source: Photos by PJ)

THE GREAT EARTHQUAKE

Deep below the mysterious earth,
A sleeping giant wakes up aloud,
To quench the fire within his girth,
Or rearrange his tectonic shroud?

Suddenly above, the ground quakes,
Numbed by panic, folks hear trouble,
Watch buildings collapse into flakes,
With loved ones buried in the rubble.

Seismic jolts attack with vengeance,
Destroy civilizations mostly ancient,
Even as royals dream of dominance,
With tall structures that are deficient.

Homes of poor built with hours of toil,
Just mud and bricks, not even mortar,
No mercy due for being on fragile soil,
Against nature, there can be no barter.

Calamities often recur to warn generations,
Are lessons taken from such destruction?
Import technology from developed nations,
Commit resources for better reconstruction.

Background: Among the major natural disasters that have constantly targeted farmers all over the world, has been the scourge of drought. India has faced one of the worst water crises in recent years. It is estimated that more than 330 million people are affected by the drought in many districts of India as the heat wave extends across the plains with temperatures exceeding 40 degrees Centigrade. Superstitions compounded with theories of global warming create more confusion for the simple farmer!

WRATH OF GOD OR GLOBAL WARMING

A solitary figure on a dry barren land,
Raises his arms to seek God's mercy,
To escape the curse of the noon sun,
Pitilessly baking his emaciated frame.

Unrolls the torn turban from his head,
To wipe away the streams of sweat,
Pouring profusely to cool his body,
But not the ever-growing anger within.

As he stares blankly at the scorched earth,
Waiting for the monsoon that never came,
Pondering idly what the future has in store,
For his family and for the whole village.

Fingers point to the callous government,
But as always, they may find a scapegoat,
Illiterate farmers barely understand politics.
What is global warming, why it's the culprit?

The village priest has convinced them all,
It is the wrath of the gods for their sins,
Appease them with gifts and sacrifices,
Rains will surely come and prosperity too.

The distant temple bells ring loud and clear
Beckoning him and others to join the rest
As mass prayers and chanting of hymns
Invoke the kindness of supernatural powers.

Background: Nepal witnessed 225 wild fires in March-April 2021 which devastated 600 hectares of forest. The environmental pollution created hazardous air quality placing Kathmandu on the list of the most polluted cities in the world.

WILD FIRES

Tiny water droplets floating in a mist,
Hiding the snowcapped peaks in a fog,
Ardent tourists cursing chances missed,
As visibility soon is worsened by smog!

Hundreds of wild fires during dry spell,
Spewing ash and chemicals into the air,
Consumed in pollution, worse than hell,
Folks with burning eyes gasp with scare.

Fragile ecosystems, forest resources lost,
Often cast-off cigarettes spread the flames,
Can human slackness be checked at a cost?
Awareness, the key to prevention one claims.

Experts blame strong winds and the heat,
While lightening at times could be a cause,
Convert policies into actions, make it a feat,
Forest conservation needs respect for laws.

THE INVISIBLE MACHINE

Human beings since time immemorial,
Wanted to rule over things terrestrial,
Conquered the sea in a maritime race,
And established a base in outer space!

God gave humans brain and creativity,
To gain knowledge, skills & capability,
And develop tools & build technology,
Ranging from radiology to climatology.

Most inventions based on nuts & bolts,
Few even produced vaccines from colts,
Modified crops to boost the agriculture,
New techniques to improve floriculture!

Of all the machines created by mankind,
The one that has turned everyone blind,
To human values like love & compassion,
Is the Hate Machine with vast allocation!

Existed ever since the dawn of civilization,
As potent as weapons of mass destruction,
Susceptible minds brainwashed by enmity,
Ready to commit any act against humanity.

Societies clash over ideological disputes,
Carnage of innocents by heartless brutes,
Millions died & millions need protection,
Is there a blueprint to stop annihilation?

ANIMAL PROPENSITIES OF MANKIND

Does a lion kill when he's not hungry?
Why rulers turn merciless when angry?
Wars destroy populations in numbers,
Even innocents are unsafe in bunkers!

Ever heard of 'road rage' in the jungle?
Rush-hour traffic might end in rumble;
Someone shoots, all ends in bloodshed,
One is heartless; another is brain-dead!

Ever seen a sea-hawk hover for a meal?
Dives to grab fish, that's his way to steal;
A lethal drone targets afar one you hate,
Humans find novel ways to assassinate!

People should know right from wrong,
Blest by God to be truthful and strong;
All animals lack this capacity to decide,
Other tiny creatures too, were denied!

In the jungle, it is 'survival of the fittest';
Of God's creations, are we the greatest?
Handful maybe, but rest, sadly, the worst,
Will His mercy save us from being cursed?

God is ever forgiving even to an offender,
If he'll change and completely surrender;
Let human values be rocks for foundation,
He'll do the rest, for our transformation!

Section-I: Loony Limericks

With a Twist from Here, There and Everywhere!

Note: Since ages, the medical profession has been considered a noble one and the lay public held doctors in high esteem. Times have changed dramatically and the very title 'Dr.' has been re-invented to suit every profession and the distinctive "white coat" is no longer the synecdoche for medical doctors.

Medical titles are increasing by leaps and bounds,
Men in white coats seen everywhere doing rounds,
Aerial doctors according to your wish,
Ready to install the latest satellite dish,
While tree surgeons do operations in open grounds!

Note: Even before the AIDS epidemic reached its peak, tourism to the fleshpots of the East ended in terrible misadventures for many.

Disguised as tourist, an actor went to the Far East,
To enjoy all the wine, the women and the feast,
Day and night, he chased pretty maids,
Thinking he won't get the dreaded AIDS,
But alas, the records show he's now deceased!

Once a rich flamboyant old Chief of Alkaria,
Returned after a pleasure trip to Kollizandria,
Boasted to pals of his rejuvenation,
But hid the agony of his micturition,
Finally, the doctor diagnosed it as gonorrhea!

Note: Tobacco has been in use in one form or the other since 3,000 BC. Today, tobacco use is the leading cause of illness, impoverishment and death (approximately 7 million deaths/year). There are 1.1 billion smokers worldwide. The illicit trade in tobacco products poses major health, economic and security concerns around the world (WHO).

(Source: Pixabay)

Once a status symbol, a cigarette case in the jacket,
Now in defiance of the grave warning on a packet,
'Smoking is injurious to your health',
Unmindful that it drains one's wealth,
Exports to the third world still a big political racket!

Note: Globally, road traffic accidents account for the death of about 1.35 million people every year. It is the leading cause of death for children and young adults aged 5-29 years. Driving under the influence of alcohol and other psycho-active substances increases the risk of accidents resulting in injuries and death (WHO).

(Source: Pixabay)

"Come on, one for the road," insists your host,
You reluctantly agree as he's better than most,
"Don't drink and drive," warned your wife,
You retorted, "I'll never take risks in life",
Too late, now you know, hovering like a ghost!

Note: Today, there is a lot of debate on the hopes and promises generated long ago by Primary Health Care (1975) and the Alma-Ata Declaration (1978) which led to the call- 'Health for All by 2000'. Sadly, even today half the world's population does not have equitable access to essential health services. Is it due to lack of political commitment or dearth of resources?

(Source: Pixabay)

'Health for All by 2000', once a famous slogan,
In some developing countries hasn't yet begun,
Programs in rich countries are feasible,
Rich ideas in poor nations, debatable,
Worse, if power comes from the barrel of a gun!

Note: This limerick is based on real life experience during the poet's tenure in the Middle East. Doctors were often embarrassed when patients requested them to also prescribe medicines for their sick household animals too (e.g. goats and donkeys)!

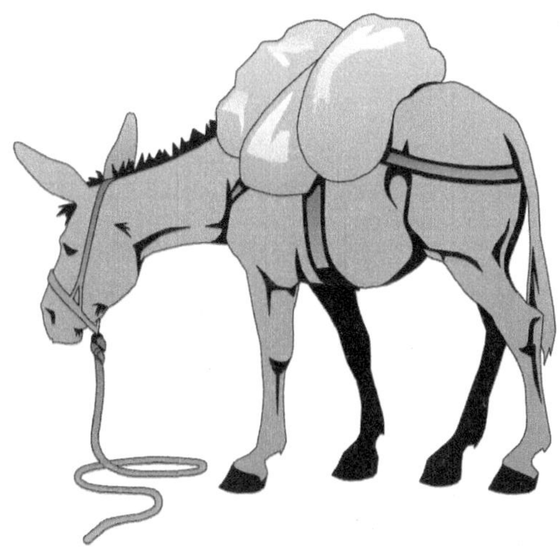

(Source: Pixabay)

Ten-year-old Asrani raced from O'Bahakey,
To the Pharmacy ten miles away in Zorkey,
"Quick, some pills for loose motion",
When asked, "Why such commotion?"
"Please", he pled, "it's for my sick donkey"!

Beside the fire station in the old city of Madras,
Lived a youth whose ears were made of brass,
When engines roared and the bells tolled,
Would twist and tremble a thousand-fold,
In despair the owners filled his ears with grass!

Grandpa said an apple a day keeps the doctor away,
Didn't work when I sneezed after playing with hay,
Grandma promptly prepared a concoction,
Pushed down my throat the terrible potion,
Does a helpless three-year-old have anything to say?

What's sauce for the goose, is sauce for the gander,
Identifying one from the other could end in blunder,
While genetic gender relies on genotype,
Somatic genetic is based on phenotype,
And no longer male or female sex, it's social gender!

Don't count your chicken much before they hatch,
Many a cricketer with butter fingers misses a catch,
Astrologers believe they are infallible,
But the future remains unpredictable,
Even marriages in heaven could end in a mismatch!

(Source: Pixabay)

Honesty is the best policy in every vocation,
Children are taught in institutes of education,
Lies deserve caning on the rump,
Fibbing leads to many a cover-up,
Yet, shamelessly repeated by every politician!

Note: When Very Important People (VIPs) get caught in a scandal it makes sensational news. Tabloids use a popular style dominated by headlines, photographs, and sensational stories which appeals to many people.

(Source: Pixabay)

Who likes to wash one's dirty linen in public?
Yet tabloids earn millions with any gimmick,
The Royals are high on the media's list,
While film stars reject with an angry fist,
But the sex life of VIPs makes one really sick!

Note: India is ranked second in the world by population. The main causes are: the birth rate is still higher than the death rate and the fertility rate is relatively higher than other countries. No wonder, every sixth person on earth could well be from India very soon!

(Source: Pixabay)

Headlines scream in all the international media,
Broadcasting the great economy boom in Asia,
All household items overseas are Chinese,
Popular car models abroad are Japanese,
Cheer up, every sixth person on earth from India!

Note: The poet's student days in Wales and Scotland had already exposed him to different accents of English spoken within the United Kingdom. Even within the Commonwealth, the English language with distinct variations in accent has been the subject of side-splitting comedy shows and jokes. Having travelled to more than 46 countries, he found that no other language can match English as the universal language for communication!

(Source: Pixabay)

The only language that's truly universal is English,
The accent identifies the Chinese from the Polish,
When you cannot hear properly, it's "Sorry",
If you step on someone's toes, still, "Sorry",
But you can never really understand the Scottish!

Note: The cult British television and radio comedy show of the 1990s, '*Goodness Gracious Me*' has made an official contribution to the English vocabulary. The Hindi word '*chuddies*', meaning undergarments, was one of 650 words in the Oxford English Dictionary's (OED) quarterly list of additions announced on March 18, 2019. The entry for '*chuddies*' cited usages dating back to 1885, but the addition, a post on the OED website made it clear, was more to do with the usage from the show. The limerick highlights the fact that the once protected English language is now at the mercy of the People of Indian Origin (PIO), with an ever-growing inclusion of native words from the subcontinent.

(Source: Pixabay)

'Goodness Gracious Me', one of those British comedies,
Where the Bhangra Muffins glorified the word 'chuddies',
Much of colonial English is from the old Empire,
No setting sun could have saved it from the mire,
No wonder, OED gets pickled by our own PIO buddies!

Note: In the Indian subcontinent, milk and milk products like yogurt are a favorite of strict vegetarians and are taken even during fasting. However, in some countries such as Ethiopia, milk and its products are forbidden during fasting, as milk is considered a non-vegetarian item. What about those South Indians who are strict vegetarians but addicted to their 'filter coffee' with plenty of milk and sugar which is rated the second best coffee in the world?

(Source: Pixabay)

Milk since ages, the best source of nourishment,
For all vegetarians the main dietary requirement,
Milk is from animals; vegans say it is taboo,
South Indians addicted to filter coffee brew,
Will find coffee sans milk a big disappointment!

Note: It is commonly said in the East that if one did not get married early, then he or she has "missed the boat"! In other words, if one fails to take advantage of an opportunity at the right time, then it becomes more difficult thereafter. But there is always hope that things may turn out on a positive note!

(Source: Pixabay)

When I was a young student, pretty and single,
All the guys in my class pursued me to mingle,
But was very committed to my studies,
Had no time for Facebook or buddies,
Now, I am forty, alone and free, did I bungle?

Did you ever hear an Elephant trumpet in English?
Or expect the Cuckoo bird to serenade in Spanish?
Pigeons always use the same frequency to coo,
Even lions roar without accent in a foreign zoo,
Only migrants from the Far East speak in Chinglish!

Do migratory birds from afar attend a crash course,
Before they fly to an alien land to study the source,
Whales don't put their calves with a nanny,
But nurture the next generation as a granny,
Why then, are tiny tots put in a playschool by force?

Digital apps are now invented to spot all kinds of bugs,
Yet, dogs are rated the best to detect bombs or drugs,
Canary birds died in mines to alert toxic leak,
When hybrid alarms fail, survival itself is bleak,
Are CCTVs and biometrics foolproof to identify thugs?